Fugitive

Fugitive Poems

John Keats

ET REMOTISSIMA PROPE

Hesperus Poetry

Hesperus Poetry
Published by Hesperus Press Limited
4 Rickett Street, London SW6 1RU
www.hesperuspress.com

Fugitive Poems first published by Hesperus Press Limited, 2004
© Hesperus Press Limited, 2004
Foreword © Andrew Motion, 2004

Designed and typeset by Fraser Muggeridge
Printed in Italy by Graphic Studio Srl

ISBN: 1-84391-077-2

All rights reserved. This book is sold subject to the condition that it shall not be resold, lent, hired out or otherwise circulated without the express prior consent of the publisher.

CONTENTS

Foreword by Andrew Motion	vii
Fugitive Poems	1
Notes	85
Index of titles and first lines	89
Biographical note	93

FOREWORD

First things first: what is 'fugitive' about John Keats? The man himself was notably courageous – someone who busily applied himself to life and work, who eagerly opposed injustice, who liked boxing and was prepared to use his own fists if necessary, and who endured the sufferings of illness with heroic fortitude. Nothing about him was (in the words of the OED) 'apt or tending to flee'. Neither was there much about his writing that we can call 'elusive' – 'slippery', yes, in its heated and panting sensuality ('slippery blisses'), and certainly preoccupied by notions of escape and impermanence, but also wonderfully real and graspable.

On the other hand his life itself was fleeting – it ended in his twenty-sixth year – and he died a refugee, in Rome, in 1821. At the time, it looked as though his reputation might be equally perishable. He had previously published three books of poetry, and the most successful had sold fewer than three hundred copies. This lack of public interest, combined with savage reviews and escalating self-doubt, led him to ask that his gravestone should not bear his name, merely the phrase 'Here lies one whose name was writ in water'. Fugitive indeed.

By the middle of the nineteenth century things had changed. Thanks partly to the advocacy of Arthur Hallam, Tennyson, and his first biographer Richard Monckton Milnes, Keats had been re-presented to the reading public: more pitiable than pugnacious, less contentious than sweetly lyrical. Many things – notably his politics – got masked or emasculated in the process, but at least he gained a name 'among the English poets'. His bones remained in exile, but the body of his work was revered.

And is still revered today – with the kind of affection shown to few writers anywhere in the world. Yet what is the focus of this affection? A few marvellous short poems, a handful of fascinating narratives, and the great odes of 1819. Although Keats wrote all his poems when he was still a young man, he was not prodigious in a Mozartian sense: many of his earliest poems (he seems to have started writing in 1814) are creaky or derivative. Furthermore, his first important poem, the sonnet on Chapman's Homer (October 1816) did not herald a steady rise to uniform excellence: many of the poems written over the next three years are slight and occasional, and occasionally slightly damaged. And then there's the matter of *Endymion* (1818), which contemporary readers find as bewildering as its first audience (though for different reasons), and the two *Hyperions* – both magnificent but both fragments.

In other words, the 'Keats canon' is at once predictable and sensible. But predictably and sensibly we must also say that it leaves a lot of golden lines unscanned – not fugitive in the sense that they willingly escape our attention, but in the way they are ousted from our view by the more perfect achievement of his best things. This is regrettable. For one thing, Keats's less famous poems often shed a bright light on the intentions and effects of his masterpieces. (The poems written on his 1818 walking tour of Scotland, for instance, especially 'There is a joy...', help us to understand the burden of the mystery he talks about in the two *Hyperions*.) For another, they refresh our sense of the whole poet by showing him in a variety of moods, and in doing so alert us to undercurrents elsewhere. When we consider the mingled affability and ambition of the sonnets he dashed off with and for Leigh Hunt we learn something about the humanity which fills the odes.

For all these reasons, a volume of Keats's 'fugitive poems' is well worth having. It also helps us to trace the arc of his development, and to appreciate its political dimension – the aspect which was effectively hushed-up by his Victorian advocates. In one of the earliest pieces included here, for example, the 'Lines Written on 29th May', we see him condemning 'infatuate Britons' who celebrate the anniversary of Charles II's restoration, and mourning the fate of Sidney, Russell and Vane – all opponents of the King who were executed for treason. This not only alerts us to convictions which underlie all his work, but also makes us think about how he eventually chose to treat those beliefs, preferring to embody them in tales, allegories and all manner of sensuous guises, rather than wag his finger. ('We hate poetry', he wrote in one of his matchless letters, that has 'too palpable a design on us.')

Alongside this, the early poems also show him testing or embracing many of the writers who helped him to find his own voice: Spenser, Chatterton, Byron. This process of self-definition is also evident in the epistles to his friends and fellow-poets George Felton Mathew ('Sweet are the pleasures...') and John Hamilton Reynolds ('Dear Reynolds...'). This latter and later poem, written shortly after finishing *Endymion* and before starting *Isabella*, soon shrugs off the grateful and affectionate mood of its opening lines (which is also the mood of a great deal of his minor work) to strike a much more challenging note. With characteristic candour and determination, Keats sees his future as a challenge – in this case, the difficulty of reconciling harsh reality with the pleasures of the imagination (or, as one might well say in the present context, with the pleasures of becoming fugitive):

> ...I was at home
> And should have been most happy – but I saw
> Too far into the sea, where every maw
> The greater on the less feeds evermore –
> But I saw too distinct into the core
> Of an eternal fierce destruction,
> And so from happiness I far was gone.

The epistle to Reynolds is one of the most powerful pieces in this collection, earning its place beside the sonnet on Chapman's Homer, '*La belle dame sans merci*', the sonnets 'When I have fears...' and 'Bright star...', and the anguished late fragment 'This living hand...'. These are the poems in which we see Keats operating at full power, organising all his components to speak in the voice we value as 'his'. But if we think of these poems as triumphant arrivals, we should also think of the other poems in this book as fascinating journeys – as his attempts to discover, define and become himself. We would not have the arrivals without the journeys. This is what makes the entire book valuable.

– Andrew Motion, 2004

Fugitive Poems

O grant that like to Peter I

O grant that like to Peter I
May like to Peter B,
And tell me, lovely Jesus, Y
This Peter went to C.

O grant that like to Peter I
May like to Peter B,
And tell me, lovely Jesus, Y
Old Jonah went to C.

(Undated)

On Peace

O Peace! and dost thou with thy presence bless
The dwellings of this war-surrounded isle,
Soothing with placid brow our late distress,
Making the triple kingdom brightly smile?
Joyful I hail thy presence, and I hail
The sweet companions that await on thee;
Complete my joy – let not my first wish fail,
Let the sweet mountain nymph thy favourite be,
With England's happiness proclaim Europa's liberty.
O Europe! let not sceptred tyrants see
That thou must shelter in thy former state;
Keep thy chains burst, and boldly say thou art free;
Give thy kings law – leave not uncurbed the great;
So with the horrors past thou'lt win thy happier fate!

(Spring 1814)[1]

Fill for me a brimming bowl

> 'What wondrous beauty! From this moment I efface
> from my mind all women' (Terence, *The Eunuch*, II.3.296)

Fill for me a brimming bowl
And let me in it drown my soul –
But put therein some drug, designed
To banish Woman from my mind;

For I want not the stream inspiring
That heats the sense with lewd desiring,
But I want as deep a draught
As e'er from Lethe's waves was quaffed,

From my despairing breast to charm
The image of the fairest form
That e'er my revelling eyes beheld,
That e'er my wandering fancy spelled.

'Tis vain! away I cannot chase
The melting softness of that face,
The beaminess of those bright eyes,
That breast – earth's only paradise.

My sight will nevermore be blessed,
For all I see has lost its zest;
Nor with delight can I explore,
The classic page, the Muse's lore.

Had she but known how beat my heart,
And with one smile relieved its smart
I should have felt a sweet relief,
I should have felt 'the joy of grief'.

Yet as the Tuscan 'mid the snow
Of Lapland dreams on sweet Arno,
Even so for ever shall she be
The halo of my memory.

(August 1814)

As from the darkening gloom a silver dove

As from the darkening gloom a silver dove
Upsoars and darts into the eastern light,
On pinions that naught moves but pure delight,
So fled thy soul into the realms above –
Regions of peace and everlasting love,
Where happy spirits, crowned with circlets bright
Of starry beam, and gloriously bedight,
Taste the high joy none but the blessed can prove.
There thou or joinest the immortal quire
In melodies that even Heaven fair
Fill with superior bliss, or, at desire
Of the omnipotent Father, cleavest the air
On holy message sent. – What pleasures higher?
Wherefore does any grief our joy impair?

(December 1814)

To Lord Byron

Byron! how sweetly sad thy melody!
Attuning still the soul to tenderness,
As if soft Pity, with unusual stress,
Had touched her plaintive lute, and thou, being by,
Hadst caught the tones, nor suffered them to die.
O'ershading sorrow doth not make thee less
Delightful: thou thy griefs dost dress
With a bright halo, shining beamily,
As when a cloud the golden moon doth veil,
Its sides are tinged with a resplendent glow,
Through the dark robe oft amber rays prevail,
And like fair veins in sable marble flow;
Still warble, dying swan! still tell the tale,
The enchanting tale, the tale of pleasing woe.

(December 1814)

Song

Tune: 'Julia to the wood robin'

Stay, ruby-breasted warbler, stay
And let me see thy sparkling eye:
O brush not yet the pearl-strung spray,
Nor bow thy pretty head to fly.

Stay while I tell thee, fluttering thing,
That thou of love an emblem art;
Yes, patient plume thy little wing,
Whilst I my thoughts to thee impart.

When summer nights the dews bestow,
And summer suns enrich the day,
Thy notes the blossoms charm to blow,
Each opes delighted at thy lay.

So when in youth the eye's dark glance
Speaks pleasure from its circle bright,
The tones of love our joys enhance,
And make superior each delight.

And when bleak storms resistless rove,
And every rural bliss destroy,
Nought comforts then the leafless grove
But thy soft note – its only joy.

E'en so the words of love beguile
When pleasure's tree no longer bears,
And draw a soft endearing smile
Amid the gloom of grief and tears.

(1815 or 1816)

To Chatterton

O Chatterton![2], how very sad thy fate!
Dear child of sorrow, son of misery,
How soon the film of death obscured that eye,
Whence genius wildly flashed, and high debate!
How soon that voice, majestic and elate,
Melted in dying murmurs! O, how nigh
Was night to thy fair morning! Thou didst die
A half-blown flower which cold blasts amate.
But this is past – thou art among the stars
Of highest heaven – to the rolling spheres
Thou sweetly singest: naught thy hymning mars,
Above the ingrate world and human fears.
On earth the good man base detraction bars
From thy fair name, and waters it with tears.

(Spring 1815)

Lines Written on 29th May,
the Anniversary of the Restoration of Charles II

Infatuate Britons, will you still proclaim
His memory, your direst, foulest shame?
Nor patriots revere?
Ah! when I hear each traitorous lying bell,
'Tis gallant Sidney's, Russell's, Vane's sad knell
That pains my wounded ear.

(May 1815)[3]

To Emma

O come, dearest Emma, the rose is full blown
And the riches of Flora are lavishly strown;
The air is all softness, and crystal the streams,
And the west is resplendently clothed in beams.

We will hasten, my fair, to the opening glades,
The quaintly carved seats, and the freshening shades,
Where the faeries are chanting their evening hymns,
And in the last sunbeam the sylph lightly swims.

And when thou art weary I'll find thee a bed
Of mosses and flowers to pillow thy head;
There, beauteous Emma, I'll sit at thy feet,
While my story of love I enraptured repeat.

So fondly I'll breathe, and so softly I'll sigh,
Thou wilt think that some amorous Zephyr is nigh –
Ah, no! – as I breathe I will press thy fair knee,
And then thou wilt know that the sigh comes from me.

Then why, lovely girl, should we lose all these blisses?
That mortal's a fool who such happiness misses.
So smile acquiescence, and give me thy hand,
With love-looking eyes, and with voice sweetly bland.

(Summer 1815?)

Give me women, wine and snuff

Give me women, wine and snuff
Until I cry out, 'Hold – enough!'
You may do so sans objection
Till the day of resurrection;
For, bless my beard, they aye shall be
My beloved trinity.

(Autumn 1815 – July 1816)

To George Felton Mathew

Sweet are the pleasures that to verse belong,
And doubly sweet a brotherhood in song;
Nor can remembrance, Mathew! bring to view
A fate more pleasing, a delight more true
Than that in which the brother poets joyed,
Who with combined powers, their wit employed
To raise a trophy to the drama's muses.
The thought of this great partnership diffuses
Over the genius-loving heart, a feeling
Of all that's high, and great, and good, and healing.

Too partial friend! fain would I follow thee
Past each horizon of fine poesy;
Fain would I echo back each pleasant note
As o'er Sicilian seas, clear anthems float
'Mong the light skimming gondolas far parted,
Just when the sun his farewell beam has darted –
But 'tis impossible, far different cares
Beckon me sternly from soft 'Lydian airs'[4],
And hold my faculties so long in thrall,
That I am oft in doubt whether at all
I shall again see Phoebus in the morning:
Or flushed Aurora in the roseate dawning!
Or a white Naiad in a rippling stream;
Or a rapt seraph in a moonlight beam;
Or again witness what with thee I've seen,
The dew by fairy feet swept from the green,
After a night of some quaint jubilee
Which every elf and fay had come to see:

When bright processions took their airy march
Beneath the curved moon's triumphal arch.

But might I now each passing moment give
To the coy muse, with me she would not live
In this dark city, nor would condescend
'Mid contradictions her delights to lend.
Should e'er the fine-eyed maid to me be kind,
Ah! surely it must be whene'er I find
Some flowery spot, sequestered, wild, romantic,
That often must have seen a poet frantic;
Where oaks, that erst the Druid knew, are growing,
And flowers, the glory of one day, are blowing;
Where the dark-leaved laburnum's drooping clusters
Reflect athwart the stream their yellow lustres,
And intertwined the cassia's arms unite,
With its own drooping buds, but very white.
Where on one side are covert branches hung,
'Mong which the nightingales have always sung
In leafy quiet; where to pry, aloof,
Atween the pillars of the sylvan roof,
Would be to find where violet beds were nestling,
And where the bee with cowslip bells was wrestling.
There must be too a ruin dark, and gloomy,
To say, 'Joy not too much in all that's bloomy.'

Yet this is vain – O Mathew, lend thy aid
To find a place where I may greet the maid –
Where we may soft humanity put on,
And sit, and rhyme, and think on Chatterton;
And that warm-hearted Shakespeare sent to meet him –
Four laurelled spirits, heavenward to entreat him.

With reverence would we speak of all the sages
Who have left streaks of light athwart their ages:
And thou shouldst moralise on Milton's blindness,
And mourn the fearful dearth of human kindness
To those who strove with the bright golden wing
Of genius, to flap away each sting
Thrown by the pitiless world. We next could tell
Of those who in the cause of freedom fell;
Of our own Alfred[5], of Helvetian Tell[6];
Of him whose name to every heart's a solace,
High-minded and unbending William Wallace[7].
While to the rugged north our musing turns,
We well might drop a tear for him, and Burns[8].

Felton! without incitements such as these,
How vain for me the niggard Muse to tease;
For thee, she will thy every dwelling grace,
And make 'a sunshine in a shady place'[9]:
For thou wast once a floweret blooming wild,
Close to the source, bright, pure, and undefiled,
Whence gush the streams of song: in happy hour
Came chaste Diana from her shady bower,
Just as the sun was from the east uprising;
And, as for him some gift she was devising,
Beheld thee, plucked thee, cast thee in the stream
To meet her glorious brother's greeting beam.
I marvel much that thou hast never told
How, from a flower, into a fish of gold
Apollo changed thee; how thou next didst seem
A black-eyed swan upon the widening stream;
And when thou first didst in that mirror trace
The placid features of a human face:

That thou hast never told thy travels strange,
And all the wonders of the mazy range
O'er pebbly crystal, and o'er golden sands;
Kissing thy daily food from Naiad's pearly hands.

(November 1815)

I am as brisk

I am as brisk
As a bottle of wisk-
Ey, and as nimble
as a milliner's thimble.

(February 1816?)

To ***

Had I a man's fair form, then might my sighs
Be echoed swiftly through that ivory shell
Thine ear, and find thy gentle heart – so well
Would passion arm me for the enterprise.
But ah! I am no knight whose foeman dies;
No cuirass glistens on my bosom's swell;
I am no happy shepherd of the dell
Whose lips have trembled with a maiden's eyes.
Yet must I dote upon thee, call thee sweet –
Sweeter by far than Hybla's honeyed roses[10]
When steeped in dew rich to intoxication.
Ah! I will taste that dew, for me 'tis meet –
And when the moon her pallid face discloses,
I'll gather some by spells and incantation.

(February 1816?)

O! how I love, on a fair summer's eve

O! how I love, on a fair summer's eve,
When streams of light pour down the golden west,
And on the balmy zephyrs tranquil rest
The silver clouds, far – far away to leave
All meaner thoughts, and take a sweet reprieve
From little cares; to find, with easy quest,
A fragrant wild, with nature's beauty dressed,
And there into delight my soul deceive.
There warm my breast with patriotic lore,
Musing on Milton's fate – on Sidney's bier[11] –
Till their stern forms before my mind arise:
Perhaps on the wing of poesy upsoar,
Full often dropping a delicious tear,
When some melodious sorrow spells mine eyes.

(Summer 1816)

On First Looking into Chapman's Homer [12]

Much have I travelled in the realms of gold,
And many goodly states and kingdoms seen;
Round many western islands have I been
Which bards in fealty to Apollo hold.
Oft of one wide expanse had I been told
That deep-browed Homer ruled as his demesne;
Yet did I never breathe its pure serene
Till I heard Chapman speak out loud and bold.
Then felt I like some watcher of the skies
When a new planet swims into his ken,
Or like stout Cortez[13] when with eagle eyes
He stared at the Pacific – and all his men
Looked at each other with a wild surmise –
Silent, upon a peak in Darien[14].

(October 1816)

To a Young Lady who Sent me a Laurel Crown

Fresh morning gusts have blown away all fear
From my glad bosom: now from gloominess
I mount for ever – not an atom less
Than the proud laurel shall content my bier.
No – by the eternal stars! or why sit here
In the sun's eye, and 'gainst my temples press
Apollo's very leaves, woven to bless
By thy white fingers and thy spirit clear.
Lo! who dares say 'Do this'? Who dares call down
My will from its high purpose? Who say 'Stand',
Or 'Go'? This very moment I would frown
On abject Caesars – not the stoutest band
Of mailed heroes should tear off my crown:
Yet would I kneel and kiss thy gentle hand.

(1816 or 1817?)

Written in Disgust of Vulgar Superstition

The church bells toll a melancholy round,
Calling the people to some other prayers,
Some other gloominess – more dreadful cares,
More hearkening to the sermon's horrid sound.
Surely the mind of man is closely bound
In some black spell, seeing that each one tears
Himself from fireside joys, and Lydian airs,
And converse high of those with glory crowned.
Still, still they toll – and I should feel a damp,
A chill as from a tomb, did I not know
That they are dying like an outburnt lamp;
That 'tis their sighing, wailing ere they go
Into oblivion – that fresh flowers will grow,
And many glories of immortal stamp.

(December 1816)

On Receiving a Laurel Crown from Leigh Hunt

Minutes are flying swiftly, and as yet
Nothing unearthly has enticed my brain
Into a delphic labyrinth – I would fain
Catch an immortal thought to pay the debt
I owe to the kind poet who has set
Upon my ambitious head a glorious gain.
Two bending laurel sprigs – 'tis nearly pain
To be conscious of such a coronet.
Still time is fleeting, and no dream arises
Gorgeous as I would have it; only I see
A trampling down of what the world most prizes,
Turbans and crowns, and blank regality –
And then I run into most wild surmises
Of all the many glories that may be.

(March 1817?)

To the Ladies who Saw me Crowned

What is there in the universal earth
More lovely than a wreath from the bay tree?
Haply a halo round the moon – a glee
Circling from three sweet pair of lips in mirth;
And haply you will say the dewy birth
Of morning roses – ripplings tenderly
Spread by the halcyon's breath upon the sea –
But these comparisons are nothing worth.
Then is there nothing in the world so fair?
The silvery tears of April? Youth of May?
Or June that breathes out life for butterflies?
No, none of these can from my favourite bear
Away the palm – yet shall it ever pay
Due reverence to your most sovereign eyes.

(March 1817?)

After dark vapours have oppressed our plains

After dark vapours have oppressed our plains
For a long dreary season, comes a day
Born of the gentle south, and clears away
From the sick heavens all unseemly stains.
The anxious month, relieving from its pains,
Takes as a long-lost right the feel of May;
The eyelids with the passing coolness play
Like rose leaves with the drip of summer rains.
And calmest thoughts come round us, as of leaves
Budding – fruit ripening in stillness – autumn suns
Smiling at eve upon the quiet sheaves –
Sweet Sappho's cheek[15] – a sleeping infant's breath –
The gradual sand that through an hourglass runs –
A woodland rivulet – a poet's death.[16]

(January 1817)

To B.R. Haydon[17]

Haydon! forgive me that I cannot speak
Definitively of these mighty things;
Forgive me that I have not eagle's wings –
That what I want I know not where to seek –
And think that I would not be over-meek
In rolling out up-followed thunderings,
Even to the steep of Heliconian springs,
Were I of ample strength for such a freak.
Think, too, that all these numbers should be thine;
Whose else? In this who touch thy vesture's hem?
For, when men stared at what was most divine
With brainless idiotism – o'erwise phlegm –
Thou hadst beheld the Hesperian shine
Of their star in the east, and gone to worship them!

(1817)

On Seeing the Elgin Marbles

My spirit is too weak – mortality
Weighs heavily on me like unwilling sleep,
And each imagined pinnacle and steep
Of godlike hardship tells me I must die
Like a sick eagle looking at the sky.
Yet 'tis a gentle luxury to weep
That I have not the cloudy winds to keep
Fresh for the opening of the morning's eye.
Such dim-conceived glories of the brain
Bring round the heart an indescribable feud;
So do these wonders a most dizzy pain,
That mingles Grecian grandeur with the rude
Wasting of old Time – with a billowy main –
A sun – a shadow of a magnitude.

(1817)

Lines

Unfelt, unheard, unseen,
I've left my little queen,
Her languid arms in silver slumber lying:
Ah! through their nestling touch,
Who – who could tell how much
There is for madness – cruel, or complying?

Those faery lids how sleek!
Those lips how moist! – they speak,
In ripest quiet, shadows of sweet sounds:
Into my fancy's ear
Melting a burden dear,
How 'Love doth know no fullness, nor no bounds.'

True! – tender monitors!
I bend unto your laws:
This sweetest day for dalliance was born!
So, without more ado,
I'll feel my heaven anew,
For all the blushing of the hasty morn.

(1817)

Lines Rhymed in a Letter Received from Oxford

The Gothic looks solemn –
The plain Doric column
Supports an old bishop and crosier;
The mouldering arch,
Shaded o'er by a larch,
Stands next door to Wilson the Hosier.

Vicè – that is, by turns –
O'er pale visages mourns
The black-tassled trencher and common hat:
The chantry boy sings,
The steeple bell rings,
And as for the Chancellor – *dominat*[18].

There are plenty of trees,
And plenty of ease,
And plenty of fat deer for parsons;
And when it is venison
Short is the benison –
Then each on a leg or thigh fastens.

(September 1817)

Think not of it, sweet one, so

Think not of it, sweet one, so –
Give it not a tear;
Sigh thou mayst, and bid it go
Any – any where.

Do not look so sad, sweet one –
Sad and fadingly;
Shed one drop then – it is gone –
O 'twas born to die!

Still so pale? then, dearest, weep –
Weep, I'll count the tears,
And each one shall be a bliss
For thee in after years.

Brighter has it left thine eyes
Than a sunny rill;
And thy whispering melodies
Are tenderer still.

Yet – as all things mourn awhile
At fleeting blisses,
E'en let us too! but be our dirge
A dirge of kisses.

(November 1817)

Nebuchadnezzar's Dream[19]

Before he went to live with owls and bats,
Nebuchadnezzar had an ugly dream,
Worse than a housewife's when she thinks her cream
Made a naumachia[20] for mice and rats.
So scared, he sent for that 'Good King of Cats[21]',
Young Daniel, who did straightway pluck the beam
From out his eye, and said, 'I do not deem
Your sceptre worth a straw – your cushion old doormats.'
A horrid nightmare similar somewhat
Of late has haunted a most valiant crew
Of loggerheads and chapmen – we are told
That any Daniel though he be a sot
Can make their lying lips turn pale of hue
By drawling out, 'Ye are that head of Gold.'

(December 1817)

Hither, hither, love

Hither, hither, love –
'Tis a shady mead –
Hither, hither, love!
Let us feed and feed!

Hither, hither, sweet –
'Tis a cowslip bed –
Hither, hither, sweet!
'Tis with dew bespread!

Hither, hither, dear –
By the breath of life –
Hither, hither, dear!
Be the summer's wife!

Though one moment's pleasure
In one moment flies –
Though the passion's treasure
In one moment dies –

Yet it has not passed –
Think how near, how near!
And while it doth last,
Think how dear, how dear!

Hither, hither, hither –
Love this boon has sent –
If I die and wither
I shall die content!

(Undated)

Stanzas

You say you love – but with a voice
Chaster than a nun's who singeth
The soft vespers to herself
While the chime bell ringeth –
O love me truly!

You say you love – but with a smile
Cold as sunrise in September,
As you were Saint Cupid's nun,
And kept his weeks of Ember –
O love me truly!

You say you love – but then your lips
Coral-tinted teach no blisses,
More than coral in the sea –
They never pout for kisses –
O love me truly!

You say you love – but then your hand
No soft squeeze for squeeze returneth;
It is like a statue's, dead –
While mine for passion burneth –
O love me truly!

O breathe a word or two of fire!
Smile, as if those words should burn me,
Squeeze as lovers should – O kiss
And in thy heart inurn me!
O love me truly!

(Undated)

Where's the poet? Show him! show him

Where's the poet? Show him! show him,
Muses nine, that I may know him!
'Tis the man who with a man
Is an equal, be he king,
Or poorest of the beggar clan,
Or any other wondrous thing
A man may be 'twixt ape and Plato.
'Tis the man who with a bird,
Wren or eagle, finds his way to
All its instincts – he hath heard
The lion's roaring, and can tell
What his horny throat expresseth,
And to him the tiger's yell
Come articulate and presseth
On his ear like mother tongue.

(1818)

When I have fears that I may cease to be

When I have fears that I may cease to be
Before my pen has gleaned my teeming brain,
Before high-piled books, in charactery,
Hold like rich garners the full-ripened grain;
When I behold, upon the night's starred face,
Huge cloudy symbols of a high romance,
And think that I may never live to trace
Their shadows, with the magic hand of chance;
And when I feel, fair creature of an hour,
That I shall never look upon thee more,
Never have relish in the faery power
Of unreflecting love – then on the shore
Of the wide world I stand alone, and think
Till love and fame to nothingness do sink.

(January 1818)

O blush not so! O blush not so!

O blush not so! O blush not so!
Or I shall think you knowing;
And if you smile the blushing while,
Then maidenheads are going.

There's a blush for 'won't', and a blush for 'shan't',
And a blush for having done it;
There's a blush for thought, and a blush for naught,
And a blush for just begun it.

O sigh not so! O sigh not so!
For it sounds of Eve's sweet pippin;
By those loosened lips you have tasted the pips
And fought in an amorous nipping.

Will you play once more at nice-cut-core,
For it only will last our youth out.
And we have the prime of the kissing time,
We have not one sweet tooth out.

There's a sigh for 'ay', and a sigh for 'nay',
And a sigh for 'I can't bear it!'
O what can be done, shall we stay or run?
O cut the sweet apple and share it!

(January 1818)

God of the meridian[22]

God of the meridian
And of the east and west,
To thee my soul is flown,
And my body is earthward pressed.
It is an awful mission,
A terrible division;
And leaves a gulf austere
To be filled with worldly fear.
Ay, when the soul is fled
To high above our head,
Affrighted do we gaze
After its airy maze,
As doth a mother wild,
When her young infant child
Is in an eagle's claws –
And is not this the cause
Of madness? – God of song,
Thou bearest me along
Through sights I scarce can bear:
O let me, let me share
With the hot lyre and thee,
The staid philosophy.
Temper my lonely hours,
And let me see thy bowers
More unalarmed!

(January 1818)

Extracts from an Opera

O were I one of the Olympian twelve[23],
Their godships should pass this into a law:
That when a man doth set himself in toil
After some beauty veiled far away,
Each step he took should make his lady's hand
More soft, more white, and her fair cheek more fair;
And for each briar berry he might eat,
A kiss should bud upon the tree of love,
And pulp, and ripen, richer every hour,
To melt away upon the traveller's lips.

* * * * *

'Daisy's Song'

The sun, with his great eye,
Sees not so much as I;
And the moon, all silver proud,
Might as well be in a cloud.

And O the spring – the spring!
I lead the life of a king!
Couched in the teeming grass,
I spy each pretty lass.

I look where no one dares,
And I stare where no one stares,
And when the night is nigh,
Lambs bleat my lullaby.

* * * * *

'Folly's Song'

When wedding fiddles are a-playing,
Huzza for folly O!
And when maidens go a-maying,
Huzza for folly O!
When a milk pail is upset,
Huzza for folly O!
And the clothes left in the wet,
Huzza for folly O!
When the barrel's set abroach,
Huzza for folly O!
When Kate Eyebrow keeps a coach,
Huzza for folly O!

* * * * *

O, I am frightened with most hateful thoughts!
Perhaps her voice is not a nightingale's,
Perhaps her teeth are not the fairest pearl;
Her eyelashes may be, for ought I know,
Not longer than the mayfly's small fan-horns;
There may not be one dimple on her hand,
And freckles many; ah! a careless nurse,
In haste to teach the little thing to walk,
May have crumped up a pair of Dian's legs,
And warped the ivory of a Juno's neck.

* * * * *

'Song'

The stranger lighted from his steed,
And ere he spake a word
He seized my lady's lily hand
And kissed it all unheard.

The stranger walked into the hall,
And ere he spake a word
He kissed my lady's cherry lips
And kissed 'em all unheard.

The stranger walked into the bower –
But my lady first did go:
Ay, hand in hand into the bower
Where my lord's roses blow.

My lady's maid had a silken scarf,
And a golden ring had she,
And a kiss from the stranger, as off he went
Again on his fair palfrey.

* * * * *

Asleep! O sleep a little while, white pearl!
And let me kneel, and let me pray to thee,
And let me call heaven's blessing on thine eyes,
And let me breathe into the happy air,
That doth enfold and touch thee all about,
Vows of my slavery, my giving up,
My sudden adoration, my great love!

(February 1818?)

Spenser! a jealous honourer of thine[24]

Spenser! a jealous honourer of thine,
A forester deep in thy midmost trees,
Did last eve ask my promise to refine
Some English that might strive thine ear to please.
But, elfin poet, 'tis impossible
For an inhabitant of wintry earth
To rise like Phoebus with a golden quill,
Fire-winged, and make a morning in his mirth.
It is impossible to escape from toil
O' the sudden and receive thy spiriting;
The flower must drink the nature of the soil
Before it can put forth its blossoming;
Be with me in the summer days, and I
Will for thine honour and his pleasure try.

(February 1818)

O thou, whose face hath felt the winter's wind

'O thou, whose face hath felt the winter's wind,
Whose eye has seen the snow clouds hung in mist,
And the black elm tops 'mong the freezing stars –
To thee the spring will be a harvest time.
O thou, whose only book has been the light
Of supreme darkness, which thou feddest on
Night after night when Phoebus was away –
To thee the spring shall be a triple morn.
O fret not after knowledge – I have none,
And yet my song comes native with the warmth.
O fret not after knowledge – I have none,
And yet the evening listens. He who saddens
At thought of idleness cannot be idle,
And he's awake who thinks himself asleep.'

(February 1818)

For there's Bishop's Teign[25]

For there's Bishop's Teign
And King's Teign
And Coomb at the clear Teign head –
Where close by the stream
You may have your cream
All spread upon barley bread.

There's Arch Brook
And there's Larch Brook,
Both turning many a mill,
And cooling the drouth
Of the salmon's mouth
And fattening his silver gill.

There is Wild Wood,
A mild hood
To the sheep on the lea o' the down,
Where the golden furze,
With its green, thin spurs,
Doth catch at the maiden's gown.

There is Newton Marsh
With its spear grass harsh –
A pleasant summer level
Where the maidens sweet
Of the Market Street
Do meet in the dusk to revel.

There's the barton rich
With dyke and ditch
And hedge for the thrush to live in,
And the hollow tree
For the buzzing bee
And a bank for the wasp to hive in.

And O, and O,
The daisies blow
And the primroses are wakened;
And the violet white
Sits in silver plight,
And the green bud's as long as the spike end.

Then who would go
Into dark Soho
And chatter with dacked-haired critics,
When he can stay
For the new-mown hay
And startle the dappled prickets?

(March 1818)

Over the hill and over the dale

Over the hill and over the dale,
And over the bourn to Dawlish[26] –
Where gingerbread wives have a scanty sale
And gingerbread nuts are smallish.

Rantipole Betty she ran down a hill
And kicked up her petticoats fairly;
Says I, 'I'll be Jack, if you will be Jill,'
So she sat on the grass debonairly.

'Here's somebody coming, here's somebody coming!'
Says I, ' 'Tis the wind at a parley.'
So without any fuss, any hawing and humming,
She lay on the grass debonairly.

'Here's somebody here and here's somebody there!'
Says I, 'Hold your tongue, you young gipsy.'
So she held her tongue and lay plump and fair,
And dead as a Venus tipsy.

O who wouldn't hie to Dawlish fair,
O who wouldn't stop in a meadow,
O who would not rumple the daisies there,
And make the wild fern for a bed do?

(March 1818)

To J.H. Reynolds, Esq.

Dear Reynolds! as last night I lay in bed,
There came before my eyes that wonted thread
Of shapes, and shadows, and remembrances,
That every other minute vex and please:
Things all disjointed come from north and south –
Two witch's eyes above a cherub's mouth,
Voltaire with casque and shield and habergeon,
And Alexander with his nightcap on;
Old Socrates a-tying his cravat,
And Hazlitt playing with Miss Edgeworth's cat;[27]
And Junius Brutus[28], pretty well so-so,
Making the best of's way towards Soho.

Few are there who escape these visitings –
Perhaps one or two whose lives have patient wings,
And through whose curtains peeps no hellish nose,
No wild-boar tushes, and no mermaid's toes,
But flowers bursting out with lusty pride,
And young Aeolian harps personified –
Some, Titian colours touched into real life –
The sacrifice goes on; the pontiff knife
Gleams in the Sun, the milk-white heifer lows,
The pipes go shrilly, the libation flows;
A white sail shows above the green-head cliff,
Moves round the point, and throws her anchor stiff.
The mariners join hymn with those on land.

You know the Enchanted Castle[29] – it doth stand
Upon a rock, on the border of a lake,
Nested in trees, which all do seem to shake

From some old magic-like Urganda's[30] sword.
O Phoebus! that I had thy sacred word
To show this castle, in fair dreaming wise,
Unto my friend, while sick and ill he lies!

You know it well enough, where it doth seem
A mossy place, a Merlin's hall, a dream;
You know the clear lake, and the little isles,
The mountains blue, and cold near neighbour rills,
All which elsewhere are but half animate;
Here do they look alive to love and hate,
To smiles and frowns; they seem a lifted mound
Above some giant, pulsing underground.

Part of the building was a chosen see,
Built by a banished santon of Chaldee;
The other part, two thousand years from him,
Was built by Cuthbert de Saint Aldebrim;
Then there's a little wing, far from the sun,
Built by a Lapland witch turned maudlin nun;
And many other juts of aged stone
Founded with many a mason devil's groan.

The doors all look as if they oped themselves,
The windows as if latched by fays and elves,
And from them comes a silver flash of light,
As from the westward of a summer's night;
Or like a beauteous woman's large blue eyes
Gone mad through olden songs and poesies.

See what is coming from the distance dim!
A golden galley all in silken trim!

Three rows of oars are lightening, moment-whiles,
Into the verdurous bosoms of those isles;
Towards the shade, under the castle wall,
It comes in silence – now 'tis hidden all.
The clarion sounds, and from a postern grate
An echo of sweet music doth create
A fear in the poor herdsman, who doth bring
His beasts to trouble the enchanted spring.
He tells of the sweet music, and the spot,
To all his friends – and they believe him not.

O that our dreamings all, of sleep or wake,
Would all their colours from the sunset take:
From something of material sublime,
Rather than shadow our own soul's daytime
In the dark void of night. For in the world
We jostle – but my flag is not unfurled
On the admiral staff – and to philosophise
I dare not yet! O, never will the prize,
High reason, and the lore of good and ill,
Be my award! Things cannot to the will
Be settled, but they tease us out of thought;
Or is it that imagination, brought
Beyond its proper bound, yet still confined,
Lost in a sort of purgatory blind,
Cannot refer to any standard law
Of either earth or heaven? – It is a flaw
In happiness to see beyond our bourn –
It forces us in summer skies to mourn,
It spoils the singing of the nightingale.

Dear Reynolds! I have a mysterious tale,
And cannot speak it: the first page I read
Upon a lampit rock of green seaweed
Among the breakers. 'Twas a quiet eve,
The rocks were silent, the wide sea did weave
An untumultuous fringe of silver foam
Along the flat brown sand; I was at home
And should have been most happy – but I saw
Too far into the sea, where every maw
The greater on the less feeds evermore –
But I saw too distinct into the core
Of an eternal fierce destruction,
And so from happiness I far was gone.
Still am I sick of it, and though today
I've gathered young spring leaves and flowers gay
Or periwinkle and wild strawberry,
Still do I that most fierce destruction see –
The shark at savage prey – the hawk at pounce –
The gentle robin, like a pard or ounce,
Ravening a worm. – Away, ye horrid moods!
Moods of one's mind! You know I hate them well.
You know I'd sooner be a clapping bell
To some Kamchatkan missionary church,
Than with these horrid moods be left in lurch.
Do you get health – and Tom the same – I'll dance,
And from detested moods in new romance
Take refuge. – Of bad lines a centaine dose
Is sure enough – and so 'here follows prose'...[31]

(March 1818)

Acrostic[32]

Give me your patience, sister, while I frame
Exact in capitals your golden name,
Or sue the fair Apollo, and he will
Rouse from his heavy slumber and instill
Great love in me for thee and poesy.
Imagine not that greatest mastery
And kingdom over all the realms of verse
Nears more to heaven in aught than when we nurse
And surety give to love and brotherhood.

Anthropophagi in Othello's mood,
Ulysses stormed, and his enchanted belt
Glow with the Muse, but they are never felt
Unbosomed so and so eternal made,
Such tender incense in their laurel shade,
To all the regent sisters of the Nine,
As this poor offering to you, sister mine.

Kind sister! ay, this third name says you are;
Enchanted has it been the Lord knows where.
And may it taste to you like good old wine –
Take you to real happiness and give
Sons, daughters and a home like honeyed hive.

(June 1818)

Sweet, sweet is the greeting of eyes

Sweet, sweet is the greeting of eyes,
And sweet is the voice in its greeting,
When adieus have grown old and goodbyes
Fade away where old Time is retreating.

Warm the nerve of a welcoming hand
And earnest a kiss on the brow,
When we meet over sea and o'er land
Where furrows are new to the plough.

(June 1818)

On Visiting the Tomb of Burns

The town, the churchyard, and the setting sun,
The clouds, the trees, the rounded hills all seem,
Though beautiful, cold – strange – as in a dream
I dreamed long ago. Now new begun
The short-lived, paly summer is but won
From winter's ague, for one hour's gleam;
Through sapphire warm, their stars do never beam –
All is cold beauty, pain is never done
For who has mind to relish, Minos-wise[33],
The real of beauty, free from that dead hue
Fickly imagination and sick pride
Cast wan upon it! Burns! with honour due
I have oft honoured thee. Great shadow, hide
Thy face! I sin against thy native skies.

(July 1818)

A Song about Myself

There was a naughty boy,
A naughty boy was he,
He would not stop at home,
He could not quiet be –
He took
In his knapsack
A book
Full of vowels
And a shirt
With some towels,
A slight cap
For nightcap,
A hair brush,
Comb ditto,
New stockings,
For old ones
Would split O!
This knapsack
Tight at's back
He rivetted close
And followed his nose
To the north,
To the north,
And followed his nose
To the north.

There was a naughty boy,
And a naughty boy was he,
For nothing would he do
But scribble poetry –

He took
An inkstand
In his hand
And a pen
Big as ten
In the other,
And away
In a pother
He ran
To the mountains
And fountains
And ghostes
And postes
And witches
And ditches
And wrote
In his coat
When the weather
Was cool –
Fear of gout –
And without
When the weather
Was warm –
Och, the charm
When we choose
To follow one's nose
To the north,
To the north,
To follow one's nose
To the north!

There was a naughty boy,
And a naughty boy was he,
He kept little fishes
In washing tubs three
In spite
Of the might
Of the maid,
Nor afraid
Of his Granny-good,
He often would
Hurly-burly
Get up early
And go
By hook or crook
To the brook
And bring home
Miller's thumb[34],
Tittlebat
Not over fat,
Minnows small
As the stall
Of a glove,
Not above
The size
Of a nice
Little baby's
Little fingers –
O he made
('Twas his trade)
Of fish a pretty kettle
A kettle –
A kettle –

Of fish a pretty kettle –
A kettle!

There was a naughty boy,
And a naughty boy was he,
He ran away to Scotland
The people for to see –
There he found
That the ground
Was as hard,
That a yard
Was as long,
That a song
Was as merry,
That a cherry
Was as red,
That lead
Was as weighty,
That fourscore
Was as eighty,
That a door
Was as wooden
As in England –
So he stood in
His shoes
And he wondered,
He wondered,
He stood in his shoes
And he wondered.

(July 1818)

To Ailsa Rock [35]

Hearken, thou craggy ocean pyramid!
Give answer by thy voice – the sea-fowls' screams!
When were thy shoulders mantled in huge streams?
When from the sun was thy broad forehead hid?
How long is't since the mighty Power bid
Thee heave to airy sleep from fathom dreams –
Sleep in the lap of thunder or sunbeams –
Or when grey clouds are thy cold coverlid?
Thou answerest not, for thou art dead asleep.
Thy life is but two dead eternities –
The last in air, the former in the deep!
First with the whales, last with the eagle skies!
Drowned wast thou till an earthquake made thee steep,
Another cannot wake thy giant size!

(July 1818)

All gentle folks who owe a grudge

All gentle folks who owe a grudge
To any living thing,
Open your ears and stay your trudge
Whilst I in dudgeon sing.

The gadfly he hath stung me sore –
O may he ne'er sting you!
But we have many a horrid bore
He may sting black and blue.

Has any here an old grey mare
With three legs all her store?
O put it to her buttocks bare
And straight she'll run on four.

Has any here a lawyer suit
Of 1743?
Take lawyer's nose and put it to't
And you the end will see.

Is there a man in parliament
Dumbfoundered in his speech?
O let his neighbour make a rent
And put one in his breech.

O Lowther[36], how much better thou
Hadst figured t'other day,
When to the folks thou mad'st a bow
And hadst no more to say.

If lucky gadfly had but ta'en
His seat upon thine arse,
And put thee to a little pain
To save thee from a worse.

Better than Southey[37] it had been,
Better than Mr D***,
Better than Wordsworth too, I ween,
Better than Mr V***[38].

Forgive me, pray, good people all
for deviating so –
In spirit sure I had a call,
And now I on will go.

Has any here a daughter fair
Too fond of reading novels,
Too apt to fall in love with care
And charming Mr Lovels[39]?

O put a gadfly to that thing
She keeps so white and pert –
I mean the finger for the ring
And it will breed a wort.

Has any here a pious spouse
Who seven times a day
Scolds as King David prayed, to chouse
And have her holy way?

O let a gadfly's little sting
Persuade her sacred tongue
That noises are a common thing,
But that her bell has rung

And as this is the *summum bo-*
Num[40] of all conquering,
I leave withouten wordes mo[41]
The gadfly's little sting.

(July 1818)

Of late two dainties were before me placed

Of late two dainties were before me placed,
Sweet, holy, pure, sacred and innocent,
From the ninth sphere to me benignly sent
That gods might know my own particlar taste.
First the soft bagpipe mourned with zealous haste,
The stranger next, with head on bosom bent,
Sighed; rueful again the piteous bagpipe went,
Again the stranger sighings fresh did waste.
O bagpipe, thou didst steal my heart away –
O stranger, thou my nerves from pipe didst charm –
O bagpipe, thou didst reassert thy sway –
Again thou, stranger, gavest me fresh alarm!
Alas! I could not choose. Ah! my poor heart,
Mumchance art thou with both obliged to part.

(July 1818)

Lines Written in the Highlands after a Visit to Burns' Country

There is a joy in footing slow across a silent plain,
Where patriot battle has been fought when glory had the gain;
There is a pleasure on the heath where Druids old have been,
Where mantles grey have rustled by and swept the nettles green;
There is a joy in every spot made known by times of old,
New to the feet, although the tale a hundred times be told;
There is a deeper joy than all, more solemn in the heart,
More parching to the tongue than all, of more divine a smart,
When weary steps forget themselves upon a pleasant turf,
Upon hot sand, or flinty road, or seashore iron scurf,
Towards the castle or the cot, where long ago was born
One who was great through mortal days, and died of fame unshorn.
Light heather bells may tremble then, but they are far away;
Woodlark may sing from sandy fern, the sun may hear his lay;
Runnels may kiss the grass on shelves and shallows clear –
But their low voices are not heard, though come on travels drear;
Blood-red the sun may set behind black mountain peaks;
Blue tides may sluice and drench their time in caves and weedy creeks;
Eagles may seem to sleep wing-wide upon the air;
Ring-doves may fly convulsed across to some high-cedared lair;
But the forgotten eye is still fast wedded to the ground,
As palmer's that, with weariness, mid-desert shrine hath found.
At such a time the soul's a child, in childhood is the brain;
Forgotten is the worldly heart – alone, it beats in vain.
Ay, if a madman could have leave to pass a healthful day
To tell his forehead's swoon and faint when first began decay,
He might make tremble many a man whose spirit had gone forth
To find a bard's low cradle place about the silent north!
Scanty the hour and few the steps beyond the bourn of care,

Beyond the sweet and bitter world – beyond it unaware;
Scanty the hour and few the steps, because a longer stay
Would bar return, and make a man forget his mortal way.
Horrible! to lose the sight of well-remembered face,
Of brother's eyes, of sister's brow, constant to every place,
Filling the air, as on we move, with portraiture intense,
More warm than those heroic tints that fill a painter's sense,
When shapes of old come striding by, and visages of old,
Locks shining black, hair scanty grey, and passions manifold.
No, no, that horror cannot be, for at the cable's length
Man feels the gentle anchor pull and gladdens in its strength –
One hour, half-idiot, he stands by mossy waterfall,
But in the very next he reads his soul's memorial.
He reads it on the mountain's height, where chance he may sit down
Upon rough marble diadem, that hill's eternal crown.
Yet be the anchor e'er so fast, room is there for a prayer.
The man may never lose his mind on mountains bleak and bare;
That he may stray league after league some great birthplace to find,
And keep his vision clear from speck, his inward sight unblind.

(July 1818)

Stanzas on Some Skulls in Beauly Abbey, near Inverness

'…*I shed no tears;*
Deep thought, or awful vision, I had none;
By thousand patty fancies I was crossed.'
(Wordsworth)[42]

'*And mocked the dead bones that laid scattered by.*'
(Shakespeare)[43]

In silent barren synod met,
Within those roofless walls where yet
The shafted arch and carved feet
Cling to the ruin,
The brethren's skulls mourn, dewy wet,
Their creed's undoing[44].

The mitred ones of Nice and Trent[45]
Were not so tongue-tied – no, they went
Hot to their councils, scarce content
With orthodoxy;
But ye, poor tongueless things, were meant
To speak by proxy.

Your chronicles no more exist,
Since Knox[46], the revolutionist,
Destroyed the work of every fist
That scrawled black letter.
Well, I'm a craniologist
And may do better!

This skull cap wore the cowl from sloth
Or discontent, perhaps from both,
And yet one day, against his oath,
He tried escaping,
For men, though idle, may be loth
To live on gaping.

A toper this! he plied his glass
More strictly than he said the mass,
And loved to see a tempting lass
Come to confession,
Letting her absolution pass
O'er fresh transgression.

This crawled through life in feebleness,
Boasting he never knew excess,
Cursing those crimes he scarce could guess,
Or feel but faintly,
With prayers that Heaven would come to bless
Men so unsaintly.

Here's a true churchman! he'd affect
Much charity, and ne'er neglect
To pray for mercy on th' elect
But thought no evil
In sending heathen, Turk and sect
All to the Devil!

Poor skull, thy fingers set ablaze,
With silver saint in golden rays,
The holy missal. Thou didst craze
'Mid bead and spangle

While others passed their idle days
In coil and wrangle.

Long time this sconce a helmet wore,
But sickness smites the conscience sore;
He broke his sword, and hither bore
His gear and plunder,
Took to the cowl – then raved and swore
At his damned blunder!

This lily-coloured skull, with all
The teeth complete, so white and small,
Belonged to one whose early pall
A lover shaded;
He died ere superstition's gall
His heart invaded.

Ha! here is 'undivulged crime!'
Despair forbade his soul to climb
Beyond this world, this mortal time
Of fevered sadness,
Until their monkish pantomime
Dazzled his madness!

A younger brother this! A man
Aspiring as a Tartart Khan,
But, curbed and baffled, he began
The trade of frightening.
It smacked of power! – and here he ran
To deal Heaven's lightning.

This idiot skull belonged to one,
A buried miser's only son,
Who, penitent, ere he'd begun
To taste of pleasure,
And hoping Heaven's dread wrath to shun,
Gave Hell his treasure.

Here is the forehead of an ape,
A robber's mark – and near the nape
That bone, fie on't, bears just the shape
Of carnal passion;
Ah! he was one for theft and rape,
In monkish fashion!

This was the porter! – he could sing,
Or dance, or play, do anything,
And what the friars bade him bring,
They ne'er were balked of
(Matters not worth remembering
And seldom talked of).

Enough! Why need I further pore?
This corner holds at least a score –
And yonder twice as many more
Of reverend brothers;
'Tis the same story o'er and o'er –
They're like the others!

(August 1818) [47]

Read me a lesson, Muse, and speak it loud

Read me a lesson, Muse, and speak it loud
Upon the top of Nevis, blind in mist!
I look into the chasms, and a shroud
Vaporous doth hide them – just so much I wist
Mankind do know of Hell. I look o'erhead,
And there is sullen mist – even so much
Mankind can tell of Heaven. Mist is spread
Before the earth, beneath me – even such,
Even so vague is man's sight of himself.
Here are the craggy stones beneath my feet –
Thus much I know, that a poor witless elf,
I tread on them – that all my eye doth meet
Is mist and crag, not only on this height,
But in the world of thought and mental might!

(August 1818)

Translated from Ronsard[48]

Nature withheld Cassandra in the skies,
For more adornment, a full thousand years;
She took their cream of beauty, fairest dyes,
And shaped and tinted her above all peers.
Meanwhile Love kept her dearly with his wings,
And underneath their shadow filled her eyes
With such a richness that the cloudy Kings
Of high Olympus uttered slavish sighs.
When from the Heavens I saw her first descend,
My heart took fire, and only burning pains…
They were my pleasures – they my life's sad end;
Love poured her beauty into my warm veins…

(September 1818)

Song

Spirit here that reignest!
Spirit here that painest!
Spirit here that burnest!
Spirit here that mournest!
Spirit! I bow
My forehead low,
Enshaded with pinions!
Spirit! I look
All passion-struck
Into thy pale dominions!

Spirit here that laughest!
Spirit here that quaffest!
Spirit here that dancest!
Noble soul that prancest!
Spirit! with thee
I join in the glee,
A-nudging the elbow of Momus[49]!
Spirit! I flush
With a Bacchanal blush
Just fresh from the banquet of Comus[50]!

(October 1818?)

Welcome joy, and welcome sorrow

> '…Under the flag
> Of each his faction, they do battle bring
> Their embryon atoms.' (Milton)[51]

Welcome joy, and welcome sorrow,
Lethe's weed and Hermes' feather;
Come today, and come tomorrow,
I do love you both together!
I love to mark sad faces in fair weather,
And hear a merry laugh amid the thunder.
Fair and foul I love together:
Meadows sweet where flames burn under,
And a giggle at a wonder;
Visage sage at pantomime,
Funeral, and steeple chime;
Infant playing with a skull;
Morning fair, and storm-wrecked hull;
Nightshade with the woodbine kissing;
Serpents in red roses hissing;
Cleopatra regal-dressed
With the aspics at her breast
Dancing music, music sad,
Both together, sane and mad;
Muses bright and Muses pale;
Sombre Saturn, Momus hale.
Laugh and sigh, and laugh again –
O the sweetness of the pain!
Muses bright and Muses pale,
Bare your faces of the veil!
Let me see! and let me write

Of the day and of the night –
Both together. Let me slake
All my thirst for sweet heartache!
Let my bower be of yew,
Interwreathed with myrtles new,
Pines and lime trees full in bloom,
And my couch a low grass tomb.

(October 1818?)

Bright star! would I were steadfast as thou art

Bright star! would I were steadfast as thou art –
Not in lone splendour hung aloft the night
And watching, with eternal lids apart,
Like nature's patient, sleepless eremite,
The moving waters at their priestlike task
Of pure ablution round earth's human shores,
Or gazing on the new soft-fallen mask
Of snow upon the mountains and the moors –
No – yet still steadfast, still unchangeable,
Pillowed upon my fair love's ripening breast,
To feel for ever its soft swell and fall,
Awake for ever in a sweet unrest,
Still, still to hear her tender-taken breath,
And so live ever – or else swoon to death.

(October 1818 – November 1819?)

Why did I laugh tonight? No voice will tell

Why did I laugh tonight? No voice will tell –
No god, no demon of severe response,
Deigns to reply from Heaven or from Hell.
Then to my human heart I turn at once –
Heart! Thou and I are here, sad and alone;
Say, wherefore did I laugh? O mortal pain!
O darkness! darkness! ever must I moan,
To question Heaven and Hell and heart in vain.
Why did I laugh? I know this being's lease
My fancy to its utmost blisses spreads;
Yet could I on this very midnight cease,
And the world's gaudy ensigns see in shreds.
Verse, fame and beauty are intense indeed,
But death intenser – death is life's high meed.

(March 1819?)

La belle dame sans merci

O what can ail thee, knight-at-arms,
Alone and palely loitering?
The sedge is withered from the lake,
And no birds sing.

O what can ail thee, knight-at-arms,
So haggard and so woebegone?
The squirrel's granary is full,
And the harvest's done.

I see a lily on thy brow,
With anguish moist and fever dew,
And on thy cheeks a fading rose
Fast withereth too.

I met a lady in the meads –
Full beautiful, a faery's child;
Her hair was long, her foot was light,
And her eyes were wild.

I made a garland for her head,
And bracelets too, and fragrant zone;
She looked at me as she did love,
And made sweet moan.

I set her on my pacing steed,
And nothing else saw all day long,
For sidelong would she bend, and sing
A faery's song.

She found me roots of relish sweet,
And honey wild, and manna dew,
And sure in language strange she said,
'I love thee true.'

She took me to her elfin grot,
And there she wept, and sighed full sore,
And there I shut her wild wild eyes
With kisses four.

And there she lulled me asleep,
And there I dreamed – Ah! woe betide! –
The latest dream I ever dreamt
On the cold hill's side.

I saw pale kings, and princes too,
Pale warriors, death-pale were they all;
They cried, '*La belle dame sans merci*
Hath thee in thrall!'

I saw their starved lips in the gloom,
With horrid warning gaped wide,
And I awoke, and found me here
On the cold hill's side.

And this is why I sojourn here,
Alone and palely loitering,
Though the sedge is withered from the lake,
And no birds sing.

(April 1819)

If by dull rhymes our English must be chained

If by dull rhymes our English must be chained,
And, like Andromeda[52], the sonnet sweet
Fettered, in spite of pained loveliness,
Let us find out, if we must be constrained,
Sandals more interwoven and complete
To fit the naked foot of poesy:
Let us inspect the lyre, and weigh the stress
Of every chord, and see what may be gained
By ear industrious, and attention meet;
Misers of sound and syllable, no less
Than Midas of his coinage, let us be
Jealous of dead leaves in the bay wreath crown;
So, if we may not let the Muse be free,
She will be bound with garlands of her own.

(April 1819?)

On Fame

'You cannot eat your cake and have it too.'
(Proverb)

How fevered is the man who cannot look
Upon his mortal days with temperate blood,
Who vexes all the leaves of his life's book,
And robs his fair name of its maidenhood;
It is as if the rose should pluck herself,
Or the ripe plum finger its misty bloom –
As if a Naiad, like a meddling elf,
Should darken her pure grot with muddy gloom.
But the rose leaves herself upon the briar,
For winds to kiss and grateful bees to feed,
And the ripe plum still wears its dim attire;
The undisturbed lake has crystal space.
Why then should man, teasing the world for grace,
Spoil his salvation for a fierce miscreed?

(April 1819)

I cry your mercy – pity – love – ay, love!

I cry your mercy – pity – love – ay, love!
Merciful love that tantalises not,
One-thoughted, never-wandering, guileless love,
Unmasked, and being seen – without a blot!
O let me have thee whole – all – all – be mine!
That shape, that fairness, that sweet minor zest
Of love, your kiss – those hands, those eyes divine,
That warm, white, lucent, million-pleasured breast –
Yourself – your soul – in pity give me all,
Withhold no atom's atom or I die –
Or living on perhaps, your wretched thrall,
Forget, in the mist of idle misery,
Life's purposes – the palate of my mind
Losing its gust, and my ambition blind!

(October 1819?)

Two or three posies

Two or three posies
With two or three simples –
Two or three noses
With two or three pimples –
Two or three wise men
And two or three ninnies –
Two or three purses
And two or three guineas –
Two or three raps
At two or three doors –
Two or three naps
Of two or three hours –
Two or three cats
And two or three mice –
Two or three sprats
At a very great price –
Two or three sandies
And two or three tabbies –
Two or three dandies
And two Mrs A*** [53] –
Two or three smiles
And two or three frowns –
Two or three miles
To two or three towns –
Two or three pegs
For two or three bonnets –
Two or three dove's eggs
To hatch into sonnets.

(May 1819?)

This living hand, now warm and capable

This living hand, now warm and capable
Of earnest grasping, would, if it were cold
And in the icy silence of the tomb,
So haunt thy days and chill thy dreaming nights
That thou wouldst wish thine own heart dry of blood
So in my veins red life might stream again,
And thou be conscience-calmed. See, here it is –
I hold it towards you.

(November – December 1819?)

In after-time, a sage of mickle lore

In after-time, a sage of mickle lore
Y-cleped Typographus the Giant took,
And did refit his limbs as heretofore,
And made him read in many a learned book,
And into many a lively legend look;
Thereby in goodly themes so training him,
That all his brutishness he quite forsook,
When meeting Artegall and Talus grim,
The one he struck stone-blind, the other's eyes wox dim.[54]

(July 1820?)

NOTES

1. Written in celebration of the signing of the Treaty of Paris, 30th May 1814.
2. Thomas Chatterton (1752–70) forged a number of poems, claiming that they were the work of an imaginary fifteenth century poet, Thomas Rowley. He committed suicide at the age of eighteen after trying, with small success, to sell his poems to magazines and publishers in London.
3. Written on 29th May 1815, when, to commemorate the Restoration of Charles II (1630–85), bells were rung all over England. Charles II had been proclaimed king on 29th May 1660, on his thirtieth birthday. Algernon Sidney (1622–83), Lord William Russell (1639–83), and Sir Henry Vane (1613–62) were looked upon as heroes by the Whigs; they were executed for treason against Charles II.
4. The Lydian style of music was characterised by soft melodies.
5. King Alfred the Great (ruled 871–99) defended Anglo-Saxon England from Viking raids.
6. William Tell is a Swiss semi-legendary hero who defied Austrian authority between the thirteenth and fourteenth centuries AD.
7. William Wallace (*c.*1270–1305) was the leader of the Scottish resistance forces during the first years of the long struggle to free Scotland from English rule at the end of the thirteenth century.
8. The Scottish Bard Robert Burns (1759–96).
9. A quotation from *The Faerie Queene* (I.iii.4, l. 8) by Edmund Spenser (1552–99).
10. In Greek times, there were at least three Sicilian cities called Hybla. Hybla Major, called Geleatis or Gereatis, on the river Symaethus, was probably the Hybla famous for its honey.
11. A reference either to Algernon Sidney (see note 3) or Sir Philip Sidney (1554–86), though most probably to the former.
12. George Chapman (1559?–1634) is the author of a celebrated translation of the Homeric epics. In October 1816, Keats spent an evening and night with his friend Charles Cowden Clarke (1787–1877) reading from a 1616 folio edition of Chapman's Homer. At ten o'clock the following morning, Keats sent a note to his friend enclosing this sonnet.
13. The explorer Hernando Cortez (1485–1547) led the Spanish in the conquest of the Aztecs in Mexico.
14. Darien is the region south and east of the Isthmus of Panama.
15. A reference to the Greek poetess Sappho (*c.*610–580 BC).
16. 'A poet's death' is probably a reference to Thomas Chatterton (see note 2).
17. Keats wrote this and the following sonnet after visiting the British Museum with his friend Benjamin Robert Haydon (1786–1846) to see the Elgin Marbles.
18. 'he rules' (Latin).

19. The poem is based on the biblical story of Nebuchadnezzar's dream and Daniel's interpretation of it (Daniel 2-4). Keats here uses the characters of the story to parody King George III (Nebuchadnezzar) and the Tory ministry (the 'valiant crew of loggerheads and chapmen'), who had been attacked by the satirist William Hone (1780-1842) – here embodied by Daniel, predicting the fall of Nebuchadnezzar's kingdom.

20. A mock naval fight.

21. A quotation from *Romeo and Juliet* (III.i.76) by William Shakespeare.

22. The invocation is to Apollo.

23. One of the twelve gods who ruled on Mount Olympus.

24. Edmund Spenser (1552-99) and his *Faerie Queene* (1590-6) were a constant source of inspiration for Keats.

25. The towns and places mentioned in the poem are situated on the north and south side of the river Teign's estuary.

26. The poem was written after a visit to Dawlish Fair. Dawlish is a small town near Teignmouth, Devon.

27. A reference to the English essayist William Hazlitt (1778-1830) and the novelist Maria Edgeworth (1767-1849).

28. A reference to the Shakespearian actor, Junius Brutus Booth (1796-1852).

29. The description of the Enchanted Castle is based on the homonymous painting by Claude (Claude Lorrain, 1604/5?-82) at the National Gallery, which probably also influenced Keats's 'Ode to a Nightingale' ('…Charmed magic casements, opening on the foam / Of perilous seas, in faery lands forlorn…').

30. Urganda la desconocida ('Urganda the Unknown') is the enchantress in the medieval chivalric romance *Amadis of Gaul*.

31. The verse letter continues in prose: 'My dear Reynolds, / In hopes of cheering you through a minute or two, I was determined nilly-willy to send you some lines, so you'll excuse the unconnected subject and careless verse. You know, I am sure, Claude's *Enchanted Castle*, and I wish you may be pleased with my remembrance of it. The rain is come on again I think with me Devonshire stands a very poor chance. I shall damn it up hill and down dale, if it keeps up to the average of six fine days in three weeks. Let me have better news of you. / Your affectionate friend / John Keats'. 'Here follows prose' is a quotation from *Twelfth Night* by William Shakespeare (II.V.156).

32. The acrostic spells out the name 'Georgiana Augusta Keats', John Keats's sister in law.

33. Minos, the legendary king of Crete, is the judge of the dead in the underworld.

34. A small freshwater fish.

35. Ailsa Craig is an island rock at the mouth of the Firth of Clyde, ten miles west of Girvan, Ayrshire, Scotland.

36. William Lowther (1787–1872), third Earl of Lonsdale, held several subordinate positions in various Tory ministries.

37. Robert Southey (1774–1843) became Poet Laureate in 1813, abandoning his early liberal ideas in favour of a much more conservative political stance, and becoming an outspoken member of the Tory party.

38. Mr D*** and Mr V*** are probably allusions to Robert Dundas, second Viscount Melville (1771–1851), and Nicholas Vansittart, Baron Bexley (1766–1851).

39. Mr Lovels is a character in *The Antiquary* (1816), a novel by Sir Walter Scott (1771–1832).

40. Literally, 'the highest good' (Latin).

41. 'Withouten wordes mo' is a Chaucerian tag meaning, 'without any more words'.

42. From *'Beloved vale!' I said* (1807), ll. 7–9.

43. *Richard III* (I.iv.33).

44. i.e. the Reformation.

45. A reference to the Councils of Nice (325, 787 AD) and of Trent (1545).

46. A reference to the Scottish Protestant leader John Knox (1505–72).

47. Written in collaboration with Charles Armitage Brown (1786–1842).

48. The poem is a translation of a sonnet by the French poet Pierre de Ronsard (1524–85).

49. Momus is the Greek god of mockery.

50. A reference to Milton's *Comus* (1634), ll. 102–4.

51. The epigraph is an adaptation from *Paradise Lost*, II, 898–903.

52. Andromeda was the daughter of Cassiopeia, Queen of Ethiopia. Cassiopeia had boasted that she was more beautiful than the Nereids, and in revenge Poseidon sent a flood and a sea monster to plague her land. To appease Poseidon, Andromeda was chained to a rock by the sea so that the monster would devour her. She was finally rescued by Perseus, who killed the monster and married her.

53. The illusion is to Mrs Abbey, the wife of Richard Abbey, the Keats children's guardian from 1810.

54. In Spenser's *Faerie Queene* (V.ii.30–54), Artegall (representing Justice) and his squire Talus destroy the simple-minded Giant, who presumes to level the world to equality. In Keats's poem, the Giant is re-educated by Typographus (the printed word) and defeats Artegall and Talus.

INDEX OF TITLES AND FIRST LINES

A Song about Myself	55
Acrostic	52
After dark vapours have oppressed our plains	27
All gentle folks who owe a grudge	60
As from the darkening gloom a silver dove	7
Before he went to live with owls and bats	33
Bright star! would I were steadfast as thou art	75
Byron! how sweetly sad thy melody!	8
Dear Reynolds! as last night I lay in bed	48
Extracts from an Opera	40
Fill for me a brimming bowl	5
For there's Bishop's Teign	45
Fresh morning gusts have blown away all fear	23
Give me women, wine and snuff	14
Give me your patience, sister, while I frame	52
God of the meridian	39
Had I a man's fair form, then might my sighs	20
Haydon! forgive me that I cannot speak	28
Hearken, thou craggy ocean pyramid!	59
Hither, hither, love	34
How fevered is the man who cannot look	80
I am as brisk	19
I cry your mercy – pity – love – ay, love!	81
If by dull rhymes our English must be chained	79
In after-time, a sage of mickle lore	84
In silent barren synod met	66
Infatuate Britons, will you still proclaim	12
La belle dame sans merci	77
Lines	30
Lines Rhymed in a Letter Received from Oxford	31

Lines Written in the Highlands	64
Lines Written on 29th May	12
Minutes are flying swiftly, and as yet	25
Much have I travelled in the realms of gold	22
My spirit is too weak – mortality	29
Nature withheld Cassandra in the skies	71
Nebuchadnezzar's Dream	33
O blush not so! O blush not so!	38
O Chatterton! how very sad thy fate!	11
O come, dearest Emma, the rose is full blown	13
O grant that like to Peter I	3
O! how I love, on a fair summer's eve	21
O Peace! and dost thou with thy presence bless	4
O thou, whose face hath felt the winter's wind	44
O were I one of the Olympian twelve	40
O what can ail thee, knight-at-arms	77
Of late two dainties were before me placed	63
On Fame	80
On First Looking into Chapman's Homer	22
On Peace	4
On Receiving a Laurel Crown from Leigh Hunt	25
On Seeing the Elgin Marbles	29
On Visiting the Tomb of Burns	54
Over the hill and over the dale	47
Read me a lesson, Muse, and speak it loud	70
Song (Spirit here that reignest!)	72
Song (Stay, ruby-breasted warbler, stay)	9
Spenser! a jealous honourer of thine	43
Spirit here that reignest!	72
Stanzas	35
Stanzas on Some Skulls in Beauly Abbey	66
Stay, ruby-breasted warbler, stay	9

Sweet are the pleasures that to verse belong	15
Sweet, sweet is the greeting of eyes	53
The church bells toll a melancholy round	24
The Gothic looks solemn	31
The town, the churchyard, and the setting sun	54
There is a joy in footing slow across a silent plain	64
There was a naughty boy	55
Think not of it, sweet one, so	32
This living hand, now warm and capable	83
To ***	20
To a Young Lady who Sent me a Laurel Crown	23
To Ailsa Rock	59
To Chatterton	11
To Emma	13
To George Felton Mathew	15
To B.R. Haydon	28
To J.H. Reynolds, Esq	48
To Lord Byron	8
To the Ladies who Saw Me Crowned	26
Translated from Ronsard	71
Two or three posies	82
Unfelt, unheard, unseen	30
Welcome joy, and welcome sorrow	73
What is there in the universal earth	26
When I have fears that I may cease to be	37
Where's the poet? Show him! show him	36
Why did I laugh tonight? No voice will tell	76
Written in Disgust of Vulgar Superstition	24
You say you love – but with a voice	35

BIOGRAPHICAL NOTE

John Keats was born in London in October 1795. In 1810 he became an apprentice to an apothecary surgeon, but gave up his apprenticeship five years later to enrole as a student at Guy's Hospital. It was around this time that he began to write poetry, his earliest efforts including 'Imitation of Spenser' and 'Ode to Apollo'. Although he qualified as an apothecary, he decided in 1816 to devote himself solely to poetry. The same year, he met Leigh Hunt, who published two of his poems, 'O Solitude' and 'On First Looking into Chapman's Homer' in his journal, *The Examiner*. Keats's first volume of poetry was published in March 1817, but after an early positive response, it received bad reviews in *Blackwood's Magazine*. Trying to conceal his hurt, he wrote to his brother George that 'I think I shall be among the English poets after my death'.

In December 1818, Keats went to live in his friend Charles Brown's house in Hampstead. It was during this time that he met and fell in love with Fanny Brawne, although they were never able to marry. The year from September 1818 saw a great outpouring of poetry, including, amongst others, *Hyperion*, *The Eve of St Agnes*, 'La belle dame sans merci', and 'Ode to a Nightingale'. This burst of activity came despite the fact that Keats was beset by financial problems, and by the winter of 1819, had become increasingly ill with tuberculosis.

His second volume of poetry, *Lamia, Isabella, The Eve of St Agnes, and other Poems* was published in July 1820 and was generally well received, although the sales were not immediately impressive. The poet Shelley invited Keats, who was by this time seriously ill, to stay with him in Italy, and in September, he and his friend Joseph Severn settled in Rome, where Keats died in February 1821.

SELECTED TITLES FROM HESPERUS PRESS

Author	Title	Foreword writer
Jane Austen	*Love and Friendship*	Fay Weldon
Aphra Behn	*The Lover's Watch*	
Charlotte Brontë	*The Green Dwarf*	Libby Purves
Anton Chekhov	*Three Years*	William Fiennes
Wilkie Collins	*Who Killed Zebedee?*	Martin Jarvis
William Congreve	*Incognita*	Peter Ackroyd
Joseph Conrad	*The Return*	Colm Tóibín
Charles Dickens	*The Haunted House*	Peter Ackroyd
Fyodor Dostoevsky	*The Double*	Jeremy Dyson
George Eliot	*Amos Barton*	Matthew Sweet
Henry Fielding	*Jonathan Wild the Great*	Peter Ackroyd
F. Scott Fitzgerald	*The Rich Boy*	John Updike
Gustave Flaubert	*Memoirs of a Madman*	Germaine Greer
E.M. Forster	*Arctic Summer*	Anita Desai
Elizabeth Gaskell	*Lois the Witch*	Jenny Uglow
Thomas Hardy	*Fellow-Townsmen*	Emma Tennant
L.P. Hartley	*Simonetta Perkins*	Margaret Drabble
Nathaniel Hawthorne	*Rappaccini's Daughter*	Simon Schama
D.H. Lawrence	*Daughters of the Vicar*	Anita Desai
Katherine Mansfield	*In a German Pension*	Linda Grant
Prosper Mérimée	*Carmen*	Philip Pullman
Sándor Petőfi	*John the Valiant*	George Szirtes
Alexander Pope	*The Rape of the Lock*	Peter Ackroyd
Robert Louis Stevenson	*Dr Jekyll and Mr Hyde*	Helen Dunmore
Leo Tolstoy	*Hadji Murat*	Colm Tóibín
Mark Twain	*Tom Sawyer, Detective*	
Oscar Wilde	*The Portrait of Mr W.H.*	Peter Ackroyd
Virginia Woolf	*Carlyle's House and Other Sketches*	Doris Lessing